Stop Playing Roulette with Your Business

How Small Businesses Fix Inconsistent Growth, Simplify Marketing, and Build Predictable Revenue

Samantha Swain Melting, Brian Borders

Stop Playing Roulette With Your Business: How Small Businesses Fix Inconsistent Growth, Simplify Marketing, and Build Predictable Revenue

Publisher

Published by Mayfield Consulting, a division of Sambria Consulting Group, LLC, Harrisburg, North Carolina

Credits

Written by: Samantha Swain Melting and Brian Borders

Edited and Produced by: Samantha Swain Melting

Design: Samantha Swain Melting

Disclaimer

This book is an independent work and is not affiliated with, endorsed by, or connected to any other organization or entity using the name “Mayfield”, “Momentum Framework.”

The concepts, frameworks, and examples presented here are based on our own experience working with small and mid-sized businesses and reflect our original thinking and approach.

This book is intended to provide practical insight and perspective. It is not a substitute for tailored business, financial, or legal advice.

All strategies should be applied based on your specific situation, goals, and constraints.

As with any business decision, results will vary.

Our goal is simple: to help business owners who feel like they are spinning their wheels gain clarity, build structure, and move forward with greater confidence.

Our Promise

At Mayfield Consulting, we believe clarity drives growth.We help small and mid-sized businesses simplify what matters, focus on results, and build momentum — one confident step at a time.

Contents

Dedication

To the business owners who never stop showing up even when the days are long, the margins are thin, and the coffee's gone cold.

To the leaders who keep building, fixing, and believing that progress is still possible.

You're the reason we do what we do.

And to our families — for the late nights and weekends filled with work, your unwavering support, and the endless patience when our passion for building Mayfield Consulting and helping others grow pulled us away from family dinners, pickleball matches, poker nights, and everything in between.

You've always believed in what we're building, and that belief means everything.

Here's to the builders, the doers, and the dreamers who keep spinning their wheels... until they don't.

— **Samantha & Brian**

A Note from the Authors

This book started as a simple idea to help small business owners thrive.

Over time, we've also had the opportunity to sit down with hundreds of customers across different industries, and hear directly what drives decisions and where businesses lose traction.

We've spent decades leading teams, building strategies, and fixing what wasn't working inside large organizations. We learned what drives results, what slows progress, and what truly motivates people. But over time, we both realized our hearts were somewhere else — with the owners and leaders who are in the trenches every day, wearing every hat, doing everything they can to build something that matters.

Building Mayfield Consulting wasn't just a career move. It was a calling. We wanted to take everything we'd learned — the wins, the hard lessons, the big-company experience

— and use it to make a real difference for smaller businesses that don't have the budgets, bandwidth, or layers of support that big brands do. We believe small businesses are the heartbeat of every community, and helping them succeed means helping families, jobs, and neighborhoods thrive.

We've seen how much clarity and confidence can change a business. Sometimes it's one conversation, one idea, or one system that reignites momentum. That's why we wrote this book — to share the lessons that have shaped us and the playbook that has helped our clients move from stuck to steady growth. This is not a book about doing more marketing. It's a book about building momentum in your business.

Our hope is that as you read, you'll see pieces of your own journey here. The frustrations, the small wins, the tough choices, and know that you're not alone in figuring it all out.

We're passionate about helping good people build great businesses, not just for the sake of profit, but because thriving businesses lift communities. And that's what drives us every single day.

Thank you for letting us share what we've learned and for trusting us to be part of your journey forward.

— Samantha & Brian

What This Book Will Help You Do

If you are running a small or mid-sized business, chances are you know the feeling. You are working harder than ever, but progress feels slower than it should.

Marketing feels scattered. Your team is busy, but growth is inconsistent. You have good ideas, but not always the time or systems to execute them.

This book was written for owners and leaders who want to change that. Inside these pages, you will learn how to:

- Simplify your marketing so it works for your team
- Build a brand that sounds real instead of robotic
- Track the few numbers that drive revenue
- Create simple systems that keep momentum moving

- Know when the right outside help can accelerate growth

You do not need a bigger budget. You do not need a massive team. You need clarity, focus, and consistent execution. That is what this book will help you build.

Introduction

Why You're Stuck (and Why It's Not Your Fault)

Running a business can feel unpredictable. You're working harder. Your team is busy. Marketing activity is happening. But growth doesn't always follow. Some months things click. Other months, nothing seems to land. It starts to feel less like a plan and more like chance.

At some point every owner asks the same question: Why does progress feel so hard?

Right now, your business might feel like a roulette wheel. You put in the effort. You launch campaigns. You try new ideas. Then you wait to see what lands.

Some weeks it works. Some weeks it doesn't. That's not a strategy. That's chance.

Are You Spinning Your Wheels?

If these sound familiar, this book will help:

- Marketing feels random
- Leads come in but follow-up is inconsistent
- Everyone is busy but growth feels slow
- Your message sounds like everyone else
- You are doing too much yourself

You're not alone. Growth doesn't stall because owners stop caring. It stalls because the business outgrows the way it used to run.

We see this every day. Smart, capable business owners who built something real. Strong products. Loyal customers. Teams who care. But somewhere along the way, momentum slipped. What once felt like progress now feels like pushing a boulder uphill.

Here's the truth: it's not because you're doing something wrong. Running a small or mid-sized business today takes more than skill and grit. It takes clarity, consistency, and systems that work. Most teams just don't have the time, bandwidth, or caffeine to juggle all that.

We get it — we've lived it. Between the two of us, we've led through growth, rebuilt what wasn't working, and helped businesses find their footing again when things got messy. And we've seen the same pattern over and over with hardworking businesses spinning their wheels, doing more but getting less traction.

We met a manufacturer doing $10M in revenue. Great product. Loyal customers. Hardworking team. But marketing was chaos. No clear priorities. No follow-up on leads. Disconnected initiatives. Six months later, growth had stalled. Not because the business was weak. Because the systems that used to work didn't scale as the business grew.

That is when we started asking a different question. Not "What marketing do you need?" But "What is slowing your momentum?" That question became the foundation for everything we do.

At Mayfield Consulting, that's exactly the cycle we help break. We simplify what matters, ditch what doesn't, and focus on what really moves the needle. This isn't a theory book or some "guru's" system. You won't find funnels, fluff, or formulas that only work for people with unlimited time and budget.

You will find practical, real-world ways to get momentum back whether you're running things yourself or ready for someone to jump in and help. Because here's the thing: growth doesn't have to feel impossible. You just need a plan that fits your size, your reality, and your goals.

The goal is simple. Stop spinning the wheel. Start building a system where results are predictable, repeatable, and within your control.

One thing we've learned after working with hundreds of businesses: most teams don't have a marketing problem. They have a clarity problem. And until that's clear, nothing else sticks.

The Mayfield Momentum Framework

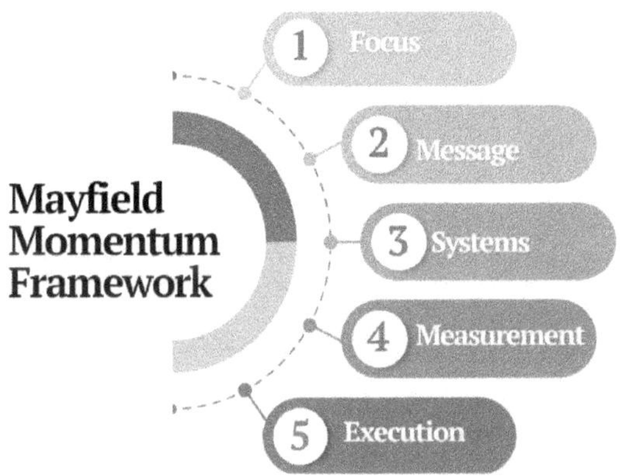

Over the years, we started noticing something interesting. Businesses rarely stall because of one big mistake. They stall because a few important pieces stop working together:

- Marketing drifts
- Messaging gets fuzzy
- Execution becomes inconsistent

When that happens, momentum disappears. That is why we use what we call The Mayfield Momentum Framework. It is a simple system that brings the essential pieces of a growing business back into alignment.

The Mayfield Momentum Framework focuses on five things:

- **Focus:** Knowing exactly what matters most right now.
- **Message:** Clearly communicating who you help and why it matters.
- **Systems:** Creating repeatable ways to execute consistently.
- **Measurement:** Tracking the few numbers that drive growth.
- **Execution:** Turning plans into action week after week.

When these five pieces work together, businesses stop spinning their wheels and start moving forward again. When one of these breaks, momentum slows. When they align, growth accelerates.

Every chapter in this book walks through one part of that system and shows you how to strengthen it inside your own business.

FROM THE MAYFIELD PLAYBOOK

The three truths we tell every client:

- You don't need a huge budget — you need focus.
- You don't need more marketing ideas — you need better execution.
- You don't need a full-time team — you need the right help, at the right time.

Everything works better when it works *together*. You can have great marketing, strong operations, and a loyal team, but if each piece is pulled from a different puzzle, you'll never see the full picture.

Growth happens when strategy, messaging, and execution align — when every part supports the next. This helps your business to run as one clear, focused system instead of a dozen disconnected efforts.

Samantha says: "Great marketing doesn't start with a budget; it starts with clarity."

Brian adds: "If you can't execute it on Monday morning, it's not a real plan."

In the next few chapters, we'll walk through the real reasons growth gets stuck, and exactly how to fix it. You'll learn how to:

- Simplify your marketing strategy so it works for your team.
- Build a brand that sounds like you, and not a corporate robot.
- Measure what matters (and stop chasing vanity metrics).
- Know when it's time to get help, and what kind of help you really need.

By the end, you'll have a clear, doable roadmap to stop spinning your wheels and start growing again with focus, confidence, and just the right amount of edge.

The Momentum Diagnostic

Is your Business Losing Traction?

Before we go further, take a quick moment to check your business momentum. Most businesses do not realize they are losing momentum until growth slows down. Take a minute and check the statements below. If several feel familiar, your business may be spinning its wheels.

- Marketing feels inconsistent or random.
- You are busy, but growth is slower than it should be.
- Leads come in, but follow-up is inconsistent.
- Your messaging sounds similar to competitors.
- Your team is working hard, but priorities change

frequently.

- You are not sure which marketing activities drive revenue.

If three or more of these apply, the issue is rarely effort. It is usually a lack of clarity, systems, or alignment.

The good news is that all three are fixable. That is exactly what the **Mayfield Momentum Framework** is designed to solve.

Chapter One

Focus - The Real Reasons Growth Gets Stuck

When businesses lose momentum, the first thing that usually disappears is clarity about what matters most. This chapter will help you identify the common patterns that slow growth and how to correct them.

***

Let's get real. Most small and mid-sized businesses don't stall because the product suddenly got worse. They stall because the business outgrew the way it used to run.

When companies are small, everything feels fast and scrappy. Decisions happen in the hallway, everyone wears three hats, and customers feel like family. Then you start growing, and the wheels start wobbling.

What once felt easy now feels messy. Marketing gets inconsistent, sales slow down, and communication turns into a game of telephone.

It's not that your team stopped caring. It's that the systems that worked with five employees don't work with fifty.

The good news? You can absolutely fix it. But first, you must see what's really happening.

1 | You're Running Without a Real Plan

Most owners know they need marketing, but it usually looks like a random playlist on shuffle.

A post here, an email there, a new logo when things get quiet.Six months later, you realize no one followed up on half the leads.

That's not a lack of hustle; it's a lack of structure. Without a simple, written plan, even great ideas fizzle out.

Action Steps

- Write down your three priorities for the next 90 days: one for awareness, one for engagement, and one for sales.

- Block one hour every other Friday to review progress.
- Ask one teammate to keep you accountable — even a simple "how's it going?" check-in keeps it moving.

Brian adds: "If it's not on a calendar, it's not a plan. It's a wish list."

2 | You're Chasing Leads Instead of Building Relationships

More leads don't always mean more business. If you've ever spent good money attracting bad fits, you already know. The best growth still comes from the people who already trust you.

Action Steps

- Identify your five happiest customers.
- Ask them for a testimonial or quick quote you can

use in sales conversations.

- Create a "refer-a-friend" email that is short, friendly, and easy to forward.

Brian adds: "You can buy clicks, but you can't buy credibility."

3 | You're Trying to Be Everywhere, and Showing Up Nowhere Consistently

Social media. Email. Trade shows. Website. PR. Some days it feels like you need a clone just to post.

Here's the truth: trying to be everywhere makes you memorable nowhere. You don't need to be on every platform. You just need to own one or two that reach your target audience.

Action Steps

- Pick your two strongest channels — the ones that bring real conversations or leads.

- Show up consistently for 90 days.
- Track what performs best and drop the rest.
- Know your audience and tailor the context to the platform and how they consume it.

Samantha says: "Focus beats frenzy every time."

4 | You're Talking About Yourself Too Much

This one stings. Most business content reads like a love letter to itself. Customers don't care that you've been around 30 years; they care what those 30 years mean for them.

Simple Swap Exercise

- Re-read your website homepage and count every "we."
- Rewrite three of them as "you."
- Ask yourself: "Would I read this if I weren't me?"

> Brian adds: "If your marketing sounds like your résumé, you're doing it wrong."

It's not enough to say what you do. You must show who you help, what problems you solve, and how your way delivers a better result.

5 | You're Measuring the Wrong Stuff

Likes, follows, clicks. They look good on paper, but they don't pay the bills. Growth lives in the numbers that tie directly to revenue: leads, quotes, repeat orders.

3×3 Momentum Check

- Track 3 metrics that drive revenue.
- Review them 3 times per month.
- Adjust 3 things (messages, offers, channels) based on what you learn.

Samantha says: "If you can't explain what success looks like, you'll never recognize it when it happens."

FROM THE MAYFIELD PLAYBOOK

When we walk into a business, we don't start with theory. We start with one question: "If we could fix what's slowing you down, what would progress look like three months from now?"

That answer becomes the plan, not a 40-page deck collecting dust, but a one-page roadmap with real accountability. Because clarity always beats complexity.

Real Example

Client Situation: Simplifying To Grow

A large company we worked with had built a strong reputation over many years. Their team was talented, their products were high quality, and their customers trusted them.

The challenge was focus.

Over time, their catalog had grown to include more than twenty different product lines. Each one required its own messaging, marketing materials, and sales conversations. The sales team struggled to explain where the company truly stood out. Marketing efforts were scattered across too many priorities, and the team was stretched thin trying to support everything at once.

Even though the company had great capabilities, the market could not clearly see what made them special.

What We Did

We worked with the leadership team to evaluate their products through three lenses: demand, profitability, and competitive advantage. Instead of trying to promote everything equally, we helped them identify the six products where they had the strongest market position and the most growth potential.

From there we simplified their marketing and sales approach. Messaging was aligned around those core offerings. Marketing focused on educating customers about those products. The sales team had a clearer story to tell about where the company truly led.

Result

Within six months, the impact was clear. Sales conversations became simpler. Marketing became easier to execute. Most importantly, revenue from those six core offerings grew significantly.

Overall sales increased by approximately twenty percent.

Lesson

Growth often accelerates when businesses stop trying to promote everything and start focusing on what they do best. Clarity creates traction.

Quick Win Checklist

- Write down your three 90-day marketing priorities.
- Focus on your two best channels.
- Rewrite one piece of copy from "we" to "you."

- Ask one happy customer for a testimonial.
- Review your top three metrics at month-end.

Chapter Takeaways

- Growth stalls when businesses lose focus.
- Marketing without structure creates inconsistency.
- Relationships outperform random lead generation.
- Focus on the few metrics that drive revenue.
- Consistency builds momentum.

Momentum Moment

If these steps got your wheels turning, you're already ahead of most. And if you're still unsure which metrics to track or which channels to focus on, that's usually a sign it's time to get another perspective.

Sometimes the best move isn't to do more. It's to bring in someone who can help you see the full picture more clearly. A trusted advisor or partner can help you connect the dots, simplify what's working, and build consistency that turns effort into lasting growth.

By now, you have probably recognized at least one place where momentum has slowed inside your business.

Maybe it is unclear priorities.Maybe it is inconsistent marketing.Maybe it is simply trying to do too many things at once.

The first step is seeing the problem. The next step is building systems that keep things moving even when your team is busy and resources are limited. That is exactly what we will tackle next.

In Chapter 2, we will show you how to create marketing systems that work even if you do not have a full marketing department.

Chapter Two

Message - Building a Brand That Doesn't Sound Like Everyone Else's

Many companies sound professional but forgettable. Their websites, emails, and marketing materials look polished, yet their message sounds just like everyone else in the industry. A strong brand does not try to sound impressive. It focuses on being clear and memorable. This chapter shows how to simplify your message, so customers quickly understand who you help and why it matters.

***

You can't outspend the "big guys", but you can out-real them. Your biggest advantage? You know your customers.

They've seen your work, shaken your hand, and maybe even called you on a Saturday. That's what makes small- and mid-sized businesses powerful. Your brand already has heart.

Now let's make sure it sounds like it.

1 | Be Real

Drop the buzzwords. Talk like you would to a customer, not a committee.

If your website says you "leverage dynamic synergies," congratulations — you just bored your audience into a nap.

Say what you mean in your own voice. Tell stories. Show results. Keep it human.

Try This Instead

- Record yourself explaining what you do to a friend or a customer and transcribe.
- Pull the best sentences straight into your website or brochure copy.

You'll appear as an authentic person, not a corporate robot.

> Samantha says: "Authenticity isn't a tactic; it's your superpower."

> Brian adds: "If it sounds like marketing copy, rewrite it until a normal person would say it out loud."

2 | A Simple Brand Story Formula

Your brand story doesn't need fireworks, but it needs clarity. Most strong brands can explain what they do in one sentence.

Use this easy formula: We help [who] solve [problem] by [how].

Example:

We help small and mid-sized manufacturers grow by fixing the gaps between marketing, operations, and execution.

If your team can repeat this sentence clearly, your brand message will stay consistent across every channel.

Action Steps

- Write your brand story in one sentence.
- Test it on three people outside your business.
- If they repeat it back accurately, you've nailed it.
- Make sure your message sounds genuine and authentic so it doesn't sound like someone else's.

Brian adds: "If your elevator pitch needs a PowerPoint, it's not an elevator pitch. Make sure it sounds like you, and not what others want to hear."

3 | Be Consistent

Every piece of communication from emails, posts, proposals, to trade-show banners should sound like it came from the same voice, even if five people wrote it.

Three-Step Brand Voice Reset

- Pick three adjectives that describe your tone (e.g., honest, approachable, confident).
- Share them with everyone who writes for your company.
- Use those words as your brand's filter for every piece of content.

Consistency builds trust. Inconsistency builds confusion.

> Samantha says: "Repetition creates recognition, so say the right thing often enough, and people start to believe it."

> Brian adds: "Your brand isn't what you say once; it's what you repeat 200 times."

4 | Show What You Stand For

People want to work with businesses that believe in something. It doesn't have to be flashy. Just honest.

Share stories about what matters to you: your team, your customers, your craft, or your community. That's what creates a connection. Not perfect graphics or fancy taglines.

Action Steps

- Post one behind-the-scenes story from your team this month.
- Share a customer success story (with permission).
- Celebrate a milestone or a lesson learned, and not just the highlight reel.

Samantha says: "Real connection starts when you stop trying to impress and start trying to relate."

Brian adds: "Trust is earned in sentences, not slogans."

FROM THE MAYFIELD PLAYBOOK

> "People don't buy from companies. They buy from people they trust to make their lives better or easier."

That's it. That's the whole play. You don't need more polish. You need more *proof.*

Real Example

Client Situation: Building a Brand That Connects

A manufacturing company approached us with a brand that had slowly become fragmented.

Over the years, marketing materials had been created by different teams, agencies, and internal leaders. As a result, the company had multiple taglines, inconsistent messaging, and visuals that did not align across channels. Customers who visited the website heard one story. Trade show materials told a different one. Sales presentations sometimes used entirely different language.

The company had a strong reputation in the industry, but their messaging did not reflect it clearly.

What We Did

Our first step was to simplify. We worked with the leadership team to clarify three core elements of their brand:

- Who they serve best
- What problems they solve
- Why their approach is different

From there we aligned messaging, visuals, and tone across every major channel. The goal was not to reinvent the company. It was to make the existing strengths easier for customers to understand.

Sales materials, marketing content, and digital channels were updated so that every touchpoint told the same story.

Result

The impact was immediate.

Customers began responding more quickly to the clearer messaging. Sales conversations became easier because the team had a shared language for explaining the company's value.

Within six months, inbound leads increased by roughly twenty-five percent.

Lesson

Clarity is not boring. When customers clearly understand who you help and how you help them, trust builds faster and growth follows.

Quick Win Checklist

- Rewrite your "About" section in plain English.
- Write your brand story using the simple formula: who / problem / how.
- Pick three adjectives that describe your brand voice and use them everywhere.

- Share one authentic story about your team or customers this month.
- Replace one piece of buzzword-heavy copy with something you'd say out loud.

Chapter Takeaways

- Strong brands communicate clearly and consistently.
- Simplicity is more powerful than buzzwords.
- Customers care more about their problems than your history.
- A clear brand story makes marketing easier across every channel.
- Authentic voices build trust faster than polished marketing language.

Momentum Moment

The best brands don't try to sound big. They sound *real.* If you're finding it hard to put your story into words or keep your message consistent, that's a signal to step back and get perspective.

A trusted outside eye can help you connect what you *do* best with what your customers *hear* best, and that's when a brand starts to really stick.

A clear brand does something powerful. It attracts the right customers, builds trust faster, and makes your marketing easier. But clarity alone is not enough. At some point, every business owner asks the same question: Is this truly working?

That is where measurement comes in.

In the next chapter, we will look at how to turn marketing from guesswork into something you can track, evaluate, and improve.

Chapter Three

Systems - Marketing Without a Team (and Without Losing Your Mind)

Most small and mid-sized businesses rely on a few good people wearing too many hats and doing their best to keep things moving. The problem is rarely effort. It is the lack of a simple system. This chapter shows how to build marketing systems that work even when your team is busy and resources are limited.

***

Most manufacturing and service businesses don't have a marketing department. Just good people wearing too many hats. You've got *Susan* posting on LinkedIn when she remembers, and *Bob* updating the website twice a year. Everyone is trying to help, but no one owns the system.

Here's the good news: you don't need a marketing department. You need a simple system you can really run.

This chapter shows you how to build one without burning out your staff or yourself.

1 | Simplify What You're Doing

Stop trying to do *all* the marketing things. Pick one or two you can do well, do them consistently, and ignore everything else for now.

You don't have to be a TikTok star or send weekly emails to win customers. Start small, stay steady.

Try This 3-Step Focus Plan

- List everything you're currently doing for marketing
- Circle the two that bring in leads, calls, or sales
- Drop or pause the rest for 30 days

Then, double down on what's working.

> Samantha says: "Consistency beats clever every single time."

> Brian adds: "If it requires dance moves or filters, probably skip it."

2 | Automate What You Can

Let's start with this. Automation is not about turning your business into a robot factory. It is about giving yourself fewer things to remember and fewer plates to spin.

Tools are your friends. Good ones quietly do their job in the background so you can focus on the work that requires a human brain. That includes scheduling apps, templates, and yes, AI.

Used the right way, automation does not replace people or thinking. It removes friction. It handles the repeatable stuff that drains time and energy so you can spend more of both on growth, creativity, and decision-making.

If something makes you think, "Why am I doing this again?" there's a good chance it can be automated.

AI is becoming a powerful tool for businesses of every size. It can help generate ideas, draft content, and automate repetitive work. But it's important to understand what it does well and where it falls short. AI will make you faster. It won't make you clearer.

AI works best when it supports thinking, not replaces it.

Use it to generate ideas.Use it to move faster.Use it to simplify execution.

But don't outsource your strategy, voice, or judgment.

Used the wrong way, AI can make your business feel more like a roulette wheel. More content. More activity. More noise. But not necessarily more results.

Used the right way, it becomes part of a system that helps you execute consistently. And consistency is what builds momentum.

FROM THE MAYFIELD PLAYBOOK

How We Use AI in Our Own Business

We do not use AI to think for us or to replace strategy, judgment, or relationships. We use it to support them.

Here are a few practical ways AI has helped us operate more efficiently and consistently:

- Expanding rough ideas into clearer drafts, outlines, or talking points so we can move faster.
- Repurposing content across channels without starting from scratch each time.
- Drafting emails, posts, or internal notes that we then refine with our own voice and experience.
- Organizing thoughts, frameworks, and client insights so nothing valuable gets lost or forgotten.
- Acting as a first-pass editor to quickly identify spelling, grammar, and clarity issues, allowing us to refine drafts faster and spend more time improving the message rather than fixing mechanics.

> AI does not replace experience. It just helps us use ours more efficiently.

What AI Is Best At

AI works best when the task is repeatable, time-consuming, or mentally draining, but not mission-critical on its own.

Good uses include:

- Scheduling content
- Creating templates
- Drafting first versions
- Summarizing notes
- Standardizing simple processes

AI works poorly when:

- You are unclear on your strategy
- You expect it to make decisions for you
- You skip review and trust it blindly

Think of automation like power tools. They are great when you know what you are building. Dangerous when you do not.

Said another way, AI works best when it accelerates thinking, not when it replaces it. Strategy, judgment, and relationships still belong to humans.

Quick Automation Wins

Start small. One or two automations can make a noticeable difference.

- Use a free scheduler like Buffer, Meta, or Later to plan posts once a week instead of daily.
- Create one reusable email template for updates, announcements, or check-ins.
- Keep a shared content calendar. A simple spreadsheet works just fine.
- Use AI to help generate ideas and direction, but then a human must edit that into something that reflects a clear vision and your authentic voice.
- Document one repeatable process and turn it into

a checklist or template.

Smart, simple systems get used. Complicated ones get abandoned.

> Brian adds: "Automation isn't cheating — it's delegation to robots that don't complain or get tired."

A Word of Caution

Automation should support clarity, not replace it. If your strategy is unclear, automation will only help you move faster in the wrong direction. Get focused first. Then automate.

Automation is not about doing more. It is about making space.

When you reduce the time spent on repeatable tasks, you create room for better thinking, stronger relationships, and more intentional growth. And when you are not sure what to automate, how to use AI responsibly, or where it adds value, that is often a sign to step back and get clear on what matters most.

The right tools, used the right way, should make your business feel lighter, not more complicated.

3 | Repurpose Everything

If you took the time to make it, squeeze every drop out of it. A single blog post or newsletter can turn into multiple assets.

Example breakdown

- 1 blog post equals 3 social posts
- 1 video becomes 1 email + 2 website clips
- 1 testimonial translates into 1 social proof quote + 1 case story

You don't need more content. You need more *use* out of the content you already have.

> Samantha says: "You worked hard to create it, so make it work hard for you."

4 | Make It Visual

People connect with faces and real stories, and not logos and stock photos. Your customers want to see the people and process behind the work.

Action Steps

- Show your team
- Show your shop floor
- Show your product doing its thing
- Replace any stock photo that feels generic or lacks your business's personality

Authenticity beats polish every time.

> Brian adds: "If your photo looks like it came from a dental brochure...and you're not a dentist, start over."

FROM THE MAYFIELD PLAYBOOK

> "If you can't explain it simply, it's too complicated to execute."

Marketing should fit your bandwidth, not break it. Simple systems get used. Complicated ones get abandoned.

Real Example

Client Situation: Customer Loyalty That Drives Sales

One client came to us focused almost entirely on generating new leads. Their marketing strategy revolved around attracting new customers, running promotions, and investing in outreach campaigns.

Meanwhile, their existing customers were quietly doing what loyal customers do: buying repeatedly.

The company had strong relationships and a history of delivering great service, but there was no structured way to nurture those relationships or reward loyalty.

Customers appreciated the company, but the business was not intentionally building on that goodwill.

What We Did

We encouraged the leadership team to shift some of their attention toward the customers who already trusted them.

Together we built a simple loyalty and relationship program. It included clear communication touchpoints, occasional rewards for repeat customers, and proactive follow-ups to strengthen relationships.

The goal was not complicated marketing. It was simply recognizing and reinforcing the value of their best customers.

Result

Within a few months, the company began to see measurable changes.

Customers who had already been buying began purchasing additional products and services. Cross-selling opportunities increased, and relationships became stronger because customers felt recognized and valued.

Cross-sell performance improved by approximately fifty percent, and customer retention strengthened at the same time.

Lesson

Growth does not always come from finding new customers. Sometimes the biggest opportunity is simply taking better care of the ones who already believe in your business. Structure creates consistency, and consistency builds loyalty.

> Samantha says: "It's not about doing more. It's about choosing what matters and doing it exceptionally well."

> Brian adds: "Systems aren't glamorous. They just work. They are what turn good ideas into consistent results"

Quick Win Checklist

- Pick one main channel and one backup.
- Create a 3-month content calendar.
- Use real photos of real people.
- Repurpose one piece of content this week.
- Set up one automation to save your sanity.

Chapter Takeaways

- Marketing does not require a large team. It requires simple, repeatable systems.
- Consistency matters more than doing everything.
- Automation should reduce friction, not replace strategy.
- Repurposing content increases the value of work you already created.

- Simple systems get used. Complicated ones get ignored.

Momentum Moment

You don't need a full team to make marketing work. You just need a system that fits your bandwidth. Start small. Stay consistent. Automate what you can.

If your efforts still feel scattered or you're unsure where to spend your time, that's a great point to bring in a partner who can help you simplify and organize what you've started.

Sometimes the smartest move isn't to do more, it's to do the right things more consistently.

Once you simplify your marketing systems, something important becomes clear. Consistency only works when your message is clear. You can post every week, automate emails, and run campaigns, but if your message sounds like everyone else in your industry, it will never stand out.

That is why the next piece of momentum is measurement.

In the next chapter, we will look at how to turn marketing into something you can measure, evaluate, and improve.

Chapter Four

Measure - Turning Marketing into Measurable Growth

Marketing becomes frustrating when businesses cannot tell what is working. Activity increases, but results remain unclear. Measurement changes that. When you track the right numbers, marketing stops feeling like guesswork and becomes something you can improve with confidence. This chapter explores how to turn marketing into growth you can measure.

***

If you can't measure it, you're guessing. Simple as that.

Marketing isn't about doing more. It's about doing what works. Busyness doesn't equal progress. It just makes you tired and stressed out.

Posts are published. Campaigns run. Emails go out. But no one knows which efforts are creating real growth. Measurement solves this problem.

When you track the right numbers, marketing stops feeling like guesswork and starts becoming a system you can improve.

1 | Track What Matters

Forget vanity metrics. Likes and clicks won't pay the bills. The only numbers worth your time are the ones that lead to sales, quotes, or repeat orders.

The 3 Rs of Measurement

- **Reach** – Are we getting in front of the right people?
- **Response** – Are they engaging or taking action?
- **Revenue** – Is that activity turning into actual dollars?

Start small — track one number from each "R" every month.

And here's an important note:Not every metric will connect directly to revenue, especially if your business sells through distributors, dealers, or channel partners. In those cases, focus on **leading indicators**, such as engagement, quote requests, dealer activity, or customer inquiries. These behaviors eventually drive sales, even if you don't see the dollars immediately.

> Samantha says: "If you can't explain what success looks like, you'll never recognize it when it happens."

> Brian adds: "Not every metric ties directly to money, but every metric should lead you closer to it."

2 | Review Monthly

Block out one hour a month — same time, same day — to really look at your numbers. No skipping. No excuses.

Monthly Review Routine

- Pull your key metrics (leads, quotes, repeat sales).
- Ask, "What moved forward this month?"
- Do more of that.
- Drop what didn't move the needle.

Consistency builds clarity, and clarity drives smarter decisions.

> Brian adds: "Think of it as an oil change for your marketing. Skip it enough, and things start to smoke."

3 | Reward Progress

Celebrate wins, even the small ones. One great testimonial. One campaign that performed. One customer who came back faster than expected. Progress builds confidence, and confidence fuels growth.

Action Steps

- Start each team meeting by naming one marketing win.
- Keep a running "Momentum List" of what's working.
- Use it to inspire your next campaign or content push.

Samantha says: "Acknowledge what's working, and it gives your team permission to keep doing it."

Brian adds: "And if the win involves spreadsheets, you'll make my day."

4 | Use Data to Make Smarter Choices

Data isn't just for dashboards. It's a decision-making tool. When you track what works, you stop guessing and start steering.

Action Steps

- Set a quarterly goal (e.g., increase repeat sales by 10%).
- Identify three actions that can directly move that number.
- Check progress monthly. Adjust and repeat.

That's how you turn marketing from a to-do list into a results engine.

FROM THE MAYFIELD PLAYBOOK

"Progress beats perfection every time.
You can't steer a parked car."

Translation: get moving, even if it's not perfect. You can adjust while you're rolling.

Real Example

Client Situation: Stabilizing Service and Customer Trust Fast

A growing service organization came to us facing an unexpected challenge.

Demand for their services had increased quickly, which should have been good news. Instead, it created pressure on their customer service team. Requests were piling up, communication was inconsistent, and employees felt overwhelmed trying to keep up.

Customers were noticing the strain. Response times slowed, and frustration started to surface in customer feedback.

The company did not lack capability. They lacked a clear way to manage the growing volume.

What We Did

We began by helping the leadership team identify the most important service metrics and communication gaps. Together we simplified internal processes, clarified responsibilities, and introduced clearer communication channels for customers.

We also helped the company strengthen their digital self-service tools so customers could resolve simple issues more easily without waiting for a response.

Result

Within four weeks, service performance began to stabilize.

Customers experienced faster responses, the team felt less overwhelmed, and the company gained better visibility into the metrics that mattered most.

Digital adoption increased by approximately five percentage points, and operational strain dropped significantly as processes became more predictable.

Lesson

When teams focus on the right metrics and simplify how work gets done, performance improves quickly. Clear priorities turn chaos into progress.

> Samantha says: "Small wins compound into big growth. Keep the scoreboard visible."
>
> Brian adds: "If you don't review results monthly, you're driving without a dashboard."

Quick Win Checklist

- Track 3 key metrics: leads, quotes, and repeat sales.
- Schedule a one-hour monthly review — and protect it.
- Drop one activity that isn't moving the needle.
- Celebrate one win with your team this week.
- Write down one specific goal for next month's metrics.

Chapter Takeaways

- Marketing should be measured by outcomes, not activity.
- Vanity metrics can distract from the numbers that drive revenue.
- A small set of clear metrics is more useful than complex dashboards.
- Reviewing results regularly improves decisions and accountability.
- Progress becomes visible when the right numbers are tracked consistently.

Momentum Moment

When you measure what matters, you stop reacting and start leading. If you're still unsure which numbers tell the real story, don't force it. Ask for feedback.

Sometimes the right conversation helps you separate what's working from what's just noise, so you can spend more time doing what moves the business forward.

When you start measuring what matters, something interesting happens. Patterns begin to appear.

You see what is working. You see what is slowing you down.And you see where your time and energy are best spent.

For many owners, this is also the moment when another realization hits. You cannot do everything alone.

In the next chapter, we will talk about when it makes sense to bring in help and how the right support can accelerate momentum instead of adding complexity.

Chapter Five

Execution - When It's Time to Get Help

Every growing business eventually reaches a limit. Opportunities increase, but time and bandwidth do not. Execution becomes harder, and progress slows. This chapter explains how the right support and outside perspective can help businesses regain momentum and move forward faster.

***

You've built something solid. You've worked hard. You've grown. But lately? It feels like you're running out of hours, ideas, and energy.

You're busy, but progress feels slower. Ideas are there, but follow-through is inconsistent. Opportunities show up, but execution doesn't always keep pace.

At some point, every business reaches this moment. Not because something is broken. Because the business has outgrown how it used to operate.

1 | Execution is the Real Differentiator

Most businesses don't fail because they lack ideas. They fail because they cannot execute those ideas consistently. Execution is not about working harder. It is about:

- Doing the right things
- In the right order
- With consistency

Week after week. That is what creates momentum.

2 | Why Execution Gets Hard

Execution breaks down for three simple reasons:

- Too many priorities

- No clear ownership
- No system for follow-through

When everything feels important, nothing gets finished. When everyone is responsible, no one is accountable. When there is no system, consistency disappears. This is where momentum slows.

3 | The Execution Gap

Most businesses live in the gap between:

- What they know they should do
- And what gets done

That gap is where growth gets lost. Closing that gap is not about motivation. It is about structure.

4| Execution Creates Momentum

Momentum is not something you wait for. It is something you build. Every time you:

- Follow up on a lead
- Publish content consistently

- Improve a process
- Have a better sales conversation

You reinforce progress. And over time, those actions compound.

5 | When It's Time to Get Help

At some point, execution hits a ceiling. Not because you're doing something wrong. Because you are doing too much. Growth plateaus aren't always obvious. They often sneak up on you.

Common signs it's time to call in backup:

- You're spending more time managing chaos than growth.
- You have great ideas but no one to execute them.
- Your team's overwhelmed, and results feel inconsistent.
- You keep saying, "We'll start next quarter."

- You're making progress, but it's slower and harder than it should be.

If you recognized more than one of these, you're not alone. This is typically the point where businesses benefit from an outside perspective. Recognizing these moments isn't weakness. It's leadership.

This is where the right support changes everything. Not by taking control, but by bringing clarity, structure, and accountability.

The right help does three things:

- Clarifies what matters most
- Simplifies how work gets done
- Keeps execution moving consistently

Sometimes you're too close to the business to see what's holding it back. That's normal. When you're juggling strategy, sales, operations, and culture, clarity gets fuzzy fast.

Bringing in help isn't about outsourcing ownership. It's about regaining perspective.

Ask yourself these 3 questions:

- What's taking up the most time, but delivering the least progress?
- What's falling through the cracks, because no one truly owns it?
- What could grow faster if someone else handled the heavy lifting?

If you can answer even one of those, you already know where help would make the biggest difference.

In our experience, the fastest progress happens when someone outside the business helps you:

- See what's really slowing things down
- Simplify priorities
- Create a plan that can be executed consistently

Because when execution becomes clear, momentum follows.

> Samantha says: "Good help doesn't replace you; it refocuses you."

Brian adds: "Even the best quarterbacks have a coach."

Momentum Check

Is your business aligned?

- **Focus:** Do you know your top priority this quarter?
- **Message:** Is your value clear to customers?
- **Systems:** Are your processes repeatable?
- **Measurement:** Are you tracking the right metrics?
- **Execution:** Are plans turning into action?

If one of these areas is weak, momentum slows.

That's where the right support can make a difference. The right support should not add complexity. It should simplify priorities, clarify direction, and help you execute consistently. It will help you get momentum back.

6 | The Mayfield Approach: Hands-On, No Fluff

We've been on both sides of the table. Leading teams, rebuilding systems, and growing businesses from the inside out.

That's why our clients trust us to step in fast, see what's really going on, and fix what's not working.

When you bring us in, we:

- **Clarify** what's working and what's wasting your time.
- **Simplify** your strategy into actionable next steps.
- **Execute** alongside your team to build repeatable momentum.

No bloated decks. No buzzwords. Just focus, follow-through, and measurable results.

> Samantha says: "We don't talk about growth alone. We build it, step by step."

Brian adds: "We don't do decks; we do results."

FROM THE MAYFIELD PLAYBOOK

Real Example

Client Situation: When It's Time to Get Help

A regional manufacturer reached a point many growing companies eventually face.

Business was strong and opportunities were increasing. Leads were coming in regularly, but the internal team did not have the bandwidth to follow up consistently.

Marketing activities were scattered across multiple initiatives, and no one had the time to coordinate them effectively. The leadership team knew growth was possible, but execution was becoming inconsistent.

In other words, the opportunity was there, but the structure to support it was not.

What We Did

We stepped in as a fractional partner to support both strategy and execution.

First, we simplified the company's marketing priorities and clarified the most valuable opportunities. Then we helped build a straightforward campaign focused on those priorities.

Just as importantly, we introduced simple systems to ensure leads were followed up consistently and communication stayed organized.

Result

Within ninety days, the changes were measurable. Quote requests increased by approximately thirty percent, and the team felt more confident managing their pipeline because the process was clearer and more consistent.

No new hires were required. The improvement came from focus, structure, and follow-through.

Lesson

Growth does not always require more people or more complexity. Often it simply requires the right systems and the right support at the right time.

Quick Win Checklist

- Make a list of what you love doing, and what drains you.
- Identify one task you could delegate this week.
- Block one hour to revisit your biggest bottleneck.
- Ask: "What would move faster if I had help?"
- Book one strategy conversation — even a short one — with someone who's been there before.

Chapter Takeaways

- Every growing business eventually reaches a limit on internal capacity.

- Outside perspective often reveals problems that are difficult to see from inside the business.
- The right support should simplify priorities, not add complexity.
- Delegating strategic work allows leaders to focus on their highest value role.
- Momentum increases when leadership focuses on what matters most.

Momentum Moment

Getting help isn't about letting go. It's about leveling up. If you're feeling stretched thin or stuck in the weeds, that's usually your cue to step back and get perspective.

The right partner won't take over. They'll help you focus, regain clarity, and move faster with less friction.

Getting help can unlock momentum, but progress does not always require a major change. Sometimes the biggest difference comes from a few small actions done consistently.

Before we wrap up, we want to share a handful of quick wins you can implement right away. Think of them as simple ways to get the flywheel turning again.

Bonus: Five Quick Wins You Can Use This Week

Sometimes momentum does not require a major strategy overhaul. Sometimes it starts with a few small actions done consistently.

The five ideas in this section are simple, practical steps that can create immediate traction. Think of them as ways to stop watching the wheel spin and start influencing where it lands.

1 | Claim or Update Your Google Business Profile

Add photos, services, and updates. Half your customers will Google you before they ever call you. Make sure what they find looks alive, not abandoned.

Action Steps:

- Spend 15 minutes this week updating your hours.
- Add at least two new recent photos.
- Respond to any recent reviews.

This is one of the fastest ways to boost credibility, and it's free.

> Brian adds: "If your last update says, 'Happy Holidays 2021,' it's time."

2 | Ask Your Best Customers for Testimonials

You already have raving fans, so let them talk. Their words will sell your business faster than any ad.

Action Steps:

- Pick three happy customers and ask for one or two sentences about what makes your business stand out.

- Post one testimonial on your website, one on social media, and one in an email signature or brochure.

Samantha says: "Real stories are more powerful than any marketing message you could write yourself."

3 | Create One Reusable Email Template

You don't need a fancy management system to stay in touch. Just a simple template you can personalize quickly.

Action Steps:

Write one short, friendly email that you can reuse for:

- sharing updates,
- announcing new products, or
- checking in with past customers.

Keep it conversational — like you're writing to a friend, not a list.

> Brian adds: "If it takes you more than 10 minutes to write it, it's too complicated."

4 | Add a "Schedule a Call" or "Schedule a Meeting" Button to Your Website

Make it easy for people to talk to you. If they have to click through three pages to find your contact form, you've already lost them.

Action Steps:

Add a simple "Book a Call" or "Schedule a Consultation" button that links directly to your calendar or a contact form.

One small change can double your inquiries overnight.

> Samantha says: "People don't want to search — they want to connect."

5 | Celebrate Your Team Online

People buy from people.

Show the faces behind your work. Highlight milestones, anniversaries, or even behind-the-scenes moments. It reminds your customers and your team that your business is built by humans who care.

Action Steps:

Share one team post this week. It could be:

- a birthday or work anniversary,
- a project win, or
- a photo of your team in action.

> Brian adds: “If you’re proud of your team, show them off. It’s good for business and morale.”

Quick Win Checklist

- Update your Google Business Profile.
- Ask for three testimonials and share them in different places.
- Create one reusable email template.
- Add a "Schedule a Call" button to your website.
- Celebrate your team online this week.

Momentum Moment

You don't have to overhaul everything to make progress. Just take one small, meaningful step each week. And if these steps reminded you of what's possible when things are focused and consistent, it might be time to think bigger.

When you align all the pieces — your strategy, marketing, and operations — momentum starts to build on its own.

By now you have seen how small changes can start building real momentum.

- A clearer message.

- Simpler systems.
- Better measurement.
- The right support when you need it.

These are not complicated ideas, but they are powerful when they work together.

Before we close, we want to leave you with one final perspective on how momentum really works in growing businesses.

Closing: You Don't Need More Ideas — You Need Momentum

We've seen it again and again: when a business finally gets focused, everything starts to click. The ideas were never the problem — execution was.

You've already built the foundation. You've done the hard work. Now it's about rhythm, clarity, and the courage to keep moving forward.

Samantha says: "You don't need to do it all at once. You just need to start."

Brian adds: "And starting next Monday still counts."

Final Thought

For a lot of business owners, growth starts to feel like a roulette wheel.

You put in the effort. You try new ideas. You make the bets. And then you wait.

Some months it works. Some months it doesn't.

That's not a strategy. That's chance. Momentum is what replaces luck with direction. Most businesses aren't stuck because they're doing nothing. They're stuck because they're relying on momentum that isn't consistent. Momentum isn't luck. It's built.

One clear message.One focused system.One step forward.

Repeated long enough, something changes.

The guesswork fades.The chaos settles.The business starts to feel steady again.

You're no longer waiting to see where the ball lands. You're building something that moves forward on purpose.

The wheel doesn't decide your outcome. You do.

Your Momentum Map

Here's how to keep building from here:

- **Focus on One Goal at a Time.** Pick one priority for the next 90 days. Don't move on until you've seen it through.

- **Simplify Every Process.** If it feels too complicated to explain, it's too complicated to execute.

- **Stay Consistent.** Block the time, protect it, and show up even when it's not exciting.

- **Track What Matters.** Follow your 3×3 Framework: three priorities, three metrics, three months.

- **Celebrate Small Wins.** Every bit of progress builds confidence, and confidence builds momentum.

Momentum Moment

If this guide sparked even one idea you can put to work right now, it's already doing its job.

Most of the businesses we work with reach a point where effort is high, but results feel inconsistent. That's usually where we come in — to simplify what's not working, double down on what is, and finally get your business running like it should.

At Mayfield Consulting, we help small and mid-sized businesses find clarity, build systems that scale, and turn stalled growth into forward motion.

You don't need more ideas. You need momentum.

Stop spinning the wheel. Start building momentum.

The Momentum Commitment

Before you finish this book, choose one action you will take this week.

- Clarify your top priority.
- Simplify one marketing effort.
- Track one meaningful metric.
- Ask one customer for feedback or a testimonial.
- Ask for help when you need it. Recognize when it is time to bring in outside perspective, guidance, or support to move faster and avoid spinning your wheels alone.

Take one step forward.

Momentum begins when action replaces hesitation.

Continue The Momentum

If this book resonated with you, you're not alone.

Most business owners don't need more ideas. They need clarity, structure, and momentum.

If you want help applying the Mayfield Momentum Framework inside your business, here are a few ways to continue:

- Join our newsletter for practical insights and real examples
- Explore additional resources at mayfieldconsulting.com
- Start a conversation if you're ready to move faster

Stop spinning the wheel. Start building momentum.

Personal Note from Samantha & Brian

Thanks for letting us share what we've learned after decades in the trenches. If this sparked even one idea to help you stop spinning your wheels and move your business forward, then it's already done its job.

We believe in real-world growth — the kind that happens when strategy meets execution.

The kind that replaces guesswork with direction.

We hope this helps you find your next move and build with real momentum.

If this book was helpful, we'd really appreciate you taking a minute to leave a quick review.

It helps other business owners who feel like they're spinning their wheels decide if this is worth their time.

About the Authors

Samantha Swain Melting

Samantha believes that every great business starts with clarity — knowing who you are, what you stand for, and how you make life better for your customers. With 30 years in executive leadership across marketing, branding, and product strategy, she's helped countless business owners move from feeling stuck to finding momentum.

As Co-Owner of Mayfield Consulting, Samantha blends big-picture strategy with practical, roll-up-your-sleeves execution. She's passionate about helping owners and leaders find their voice, sharpen their story, and build brands that really connect with people — not just sell to them. Her approach is grounded in empathy, experience, and the belief that small businesses can make a big impact when they focus on what really matters.

Connect with Samantha here to get her tips, insights, and practical guidance on turning unpredictable growth into consistent momentum.

in linkedin.com/samanthamelting

Brian Borders

Brian has spent more than 30 years helping businesses cut through the noise, fix what's broken, and focus on what drives results. He's known for his straightforward approach with no fluff, no jargon, just practical strategies that work in the real world.

As Co-Owner of Mayfield Consulting, Brian helps leaders get unstuck by simplifying operations, tightening execution, and making sure the right things get done — the right way. He believes that progress beats perfection, and that most business problems aren't as complicated as people make them. (As he likes to say, "We don't do decks. We do results.")

Connect with Brian here to get his insights, perspective, and real-world guidance on what it takes to run and grow a business.

in linkedin.com/brianborders

The Momentum Toolkit: Practical Tools You Can Use Today

This section is designed to be used as a reference. You don't need to read it all at once.

- 90-Day Growth Roadmap
- Marketing Funnel Diagnostic
- Testimonial Request Script
- Post-Acquisition Jumpstart Guide

Download the complete toolkit and additional templates at: **mayfieldconsulting.com/resource**

***

90-Day Business Quick Wins Roadmap

Big growth starts with small wins. This roadmap shows you what to tackle first, so you're building momentum step by step over the next 90 days instead of stalling out with scattered efforts.

Quick Wins (0–30 days)

- Collect and highlight 3–5 client testimonials.
- Add clear CTA buttons to your website.
- Post consistently (3–4x/week).
- Send a branded welcome email.

Build Momentum (31–60 days)

- Launch a simple lead magnet.
- Run a small ad campaign.
- Create a 3-part email nurture sequence.

- Share behind-the-scenes or customer stories.

Grow & Scale (61–90 days)

- Launch a referral program.
- Add retargeting ads.
- Create deeper content (blogs, videos, guides).
- Review performance and adjust.

So what?

Most businesses fail because they don't know what to do first. This roadmap prioritizes wins in the right order, so you're building traction, not just running in circles.

***

Marketing That Converts – Mini Playbook

This checklist is designed to help you quickly assess whether your marketing is working as a system, not a set of disconnected activities. You do not need to be perfect in every area. The goal is to identify gaps, prioritize fixes, and create momentum.

If you check most of these boxes, your funnel is doing its job. If not, this gives you a clear place to start.

Top of Funnel | Awareness

This stage is about visibility and clarity. People cannot choose you if they do not understand what you do or why it matters.

- You show up regularly in front of new people. Consistency matters more than frequency. Showing up weekly beats posting sporadically.
- You offer something useful, not just promotional content. Education, insight, or perspective builds interest faster than sales messages.
- Your content explains what you do in 10 seconds

or less. If someone cannot quickly understand how you help, they will move on.

Middle of Funnel | Build Trust

This stage is where curiosity turns into confidence. Most businesses lose momentum here.

- You follow up when someone shows interest. Interest fades quickly. Timely follow-up keeps conversations moving.

- You have a lead magnet or nurture sequence. This can be simple. A checklist, short guide, or helpful email series works.

- You share proof and behind-the-scenes content. Testimonials, stories, and process build trust better than claims.

Bottom of Funnel | Make It Easy

This stage removes friction. The easier the next step, the more likely people are to take it.

- You offer a clear next step, such as booking a call

or requesting a quote. Never assume people know what to do next.

- The next step is simple and specific. Fewer clicks. Clear language. No guessing.
- You share a quick win or proof point to close the gap. A short success story or result reassures people they are making a smart decision.

How to Use This Checklist

- If you are weak at the top, focus on clarity and consistency.
- If the middle is leaky, strengthen follow-up and proof.
- If the bottom is slow, simplify the next step.

Marketing that converts does not happen by chance. By converts, we mean turning interest into action, where someone moves from awareness to taking a real next step. It works when every part of the funnel supports the next and nothing is left to guesswork.

If you want help designing the system, plugging the leaks, and measuring what works, this is where the right perspective can make all the difference.

***

Fix Your Funnel – Quick Diagnostic

What's a Funnel, Really?

Think of your funnel as the path people take from first noticing you to buying.

- **Top of Funnel (Awareness):** This is where people first hear about you. Social posts, ads, word-of-mouth, networking — it's how they discover you exist.

- **Middle of Funnel (Trust):** Now they're curious, but not ready to buy. This is where you earn credibility through proof — testimonials, reviews, helpful content, and follow-up.

- **Bottom of Funnel (Action):** This is the decision point. They're weighing whether to buy from you or someone else. Clear offers, easy next steps, and urgency close the gap.

If your funnel leaks at any stage, you lose customers before they ever get to "yes."

Checklist

Here is a checklist to help you understand where your gaps are.

Top of Funnel – Awareness

- Website is clear about who you are and what you do.
- Social posts speak to customer problems (not just promotions).
- You're targeting the right audience (not just "everyone").

Middle of Funnel – Trust

- You use proof points (testimonials, reviews, results).
- You follow up when people engage (clicks, downloads, inquiries).
- Emails feel human — not robotic.

Bottom of Funnel – Action

- CTAs (Call-To-Action) are clear and everywhere.
- You've eliminated unnecessary steps between "I'm interested" and "Let's go."
- People have a reason to act now.

Most funnels aren't broken — they're leaking.

So what?

If leads are coming in but not converting, you're leaving money on the table. This checklist shows where people fall out and how to plug those leaks for faster revenue growth.

***

Testimonial Request Script

Most customers are happy to help. They just need you to make it easy and specific.

Use one of the scripts below as written or adapt it to your voice.

Option 1

> Hi [Name],
>
> I hope you're doing well. I wanted to reach out and thank you again for working with us. We really enjoyed partnering with you on [project or service].
>
> We're continuing to grow our business, and feedback from customers like you helps others understand what it's really like to work with us.

If you're open to it, would you be willing to share a short testimonial? A few sentences are more than enough. What problem were you trying to solve? What stood out about working with us? Any result or outcome you've seen?

No pressure at all. I just wanted to ask.Th anks again, and I appreciate your support.

Best,[Your Name]

Option 2

Hi [Name],

We're collecting a few customer testimonials and thought of you. If you're open to it, here are two quick prompts you can respond to. Bullet points are fine. What was going on in your business before we worked together? What changed or improved after?

Thank you so much. We truly appreciate it.

Best,[Your Name]

Helpful Tip

Ask for testimonials right after:

- A successful project
- A positive email or compliment
- A milestone or win

That's when feedback is most genuine and easiest to capture.

***

The Post-Acquisition Jumpstart

Buying a business is exciting — but it's also risky. The truth is that most acquisitions don't fail because of the deal terms... they fail in the first 90 days after closing. Customers get nervous, employees feel uncertain, and new owners rush to change too much too soon.

This guide is your **90-day survival kit**. It gives you a clear roadmap to:

- Nail your messaging so customers and employees trust the transition.
- Protect and retain the right people.
- Get visible fast without overwhelming your team.
- Score quick wins that build momentum.
- Avoid the common mistakes that sink new owners.

Why the First 90 Days Matter

Most acquisitions fail not because of financials, but because of what happens *after* the deal. The first 90 days set the tone — for employees, customers, and the market. Get them right, and you protect value and create momentum. Rush or overlook them, and small cracks turn into expensive problems.

This playbook helps you lead with clarity, confidence, and purpose from Day One.

Week 1: Nail the Message

Goal: Communicate clearly and consistently — inside and out.

Key Actions:

- Craft one simple message: What's changing, what's not, and why it matters.
- Hold a company-wide kickoff meeting (or video message). Keep it transparent, upbeat, and realistic.
- Meet with key managers or team leads — hear their perspective and make sure they can repeat

your message.

- Draft 2–3 short statements you can use for customers, vendors, and partners.
- Update your website, email signatures, and voicemail to reflect new ownership (no long explanations — just clarity and continuity).

Watch For:

- Over-communication beats confusion.
- Don't promise big changes too early. Stability first.

Weeks 2 – 4: Retain the Right People

Goal: Protect the relationships and knowledge that make the business run.

Key Actions:

- Identify your top 20% of employees who carry

80% of value — connect personally.

- Review compensation, incentives, and workload to retain key players.
- Schedule informal one-on-one check-ins to understand morale and pain points.
- Communicate your leadership style and expectations. People don't fear change — they fear uncertainty.
- Review vendor and partner relationships — confirm contracts, payment terms, and service expectations.

Watch For:

- Hidden influencers — the employees everyone else looks to for cues.
- Don't restructure too soon. Understand before you change.

Weeks 5 – 8: Get Visible Fast

Goal: Reassure customers, the market, and the community that the business is stable and thriving.

Key Actions:

- Send a customer announcement — short, confident, and focused on continuity.
- Post a "New Chapter" update on LinkedIn and the company website.
- Visit or call your top 10 customers personally. Ask, "What's working? What can we improve?"
- Audit all public-facing materials (brochures, listings, reviews) — update ownership info and contact details.
- Strengthen your digital footprint: consistent posts, refreshed photos, and clear messaging.

Watch For:

- Radio silence = uncertainty. Stay visible and steady.
- Keep messaging positive, not self-congratulatory. This is about continuity and growth.

Weeks 9 – 12: Make Quick Wins Real

Goal: Build early momentum and demonstrate progress.

Key Actions:

- Identify one process improvement you can implement quickly (e.g., faster response times, simpler quoting, cleaner workflows).
- Celebrate an internal or customer success story — share it in meetings or social posts.
- Review pricing, customer experience, and feedback channels — find one "easy fix" that creates visible impact.
- Evaluate your marketing and lead flow. Where can you show improvement fast?

- Align your leadership team around one short-term goal everyone can rally behind.

Watch For:

- Don't change everything at once. Pick high-impact, low-disruption wins.
- Share credit publicly — "the team" always wins the first 90 days.

Month 3: Set the Foundation for Growth

Goal: Transition from stabilization to strategy.

Key Actions:

- Reassess priorities based on what you've learned.
- Identify 2–3 key initiatives for the next quarter (e.g., customer retention, marketing refresh, team development).
- Evaluate roles, talent gaps, and resource needs.

- Schedule a strategy working session (90 minutes) to build your 6-month roadmap.
- Establish rhythms: monthly leadership meetings, quarterly reviews, and consistent internal updates.

Watch For:

- Don't overcommit. Sustainable growth starts with clarity and structure.
- Use what you've learned — now you know the business, the people, and the market better.

Common Mistakes to Avoid:

- Talking before listening — slow down, learn the culture.
- Changing processes too early — what looks inefficient might be intentional.
- Ignoring the team — culture changes faster than

systems.

- Under-communicating with customers — silence causes doubt.
- Skipping the quick wins — early wins buy long-term trust.

www.ingramcontent.com/pod-product-compliance
Lightning Source LLC
LaVergne TN
LVHW020640100826
845148LV00012B/2266

* 9 7 9 8 2 3 4 0 7 5 3 5 2 *